THE WILL TO CARRY ON

CHALLENGES OF YOUNG ATHLETES

TaRhonda White

authorHOUSE®

AuthorHouse™
1663 Liberty Drive
Bloomington, IN 47403
www.authorhouse.com
Phone: 1-800-839-8640

Published by AuthorHouse 3/26/2012

ISBN: 9781468558111 (sc)
ISBN: 9781468558128 (hc)
ISBN: 9781468558135 (e)

Library of Congress Control Number: 2012903933

Cover Design: Ana Storer
Conceptual Cover Design: TaRhonda White
Artwork Design: Ana Storer
Conceptual Artwork Design: TaRhonda White
Editor: Arlene W. Robinson
Back Cover Photograph: Xamilia Alston

This book is dedicated to
Ryan Francis, the friend who changed my heart
&
Marvin Haynes, the man who changed my life

CONTENTS

Special Thanks And Acknowledgements

Never in a million years could anyone have told me that I would come to this moment in my life; but I am here, and I want to start by giving thanks.

Heavenly Father, you are my everything. Without your guidance and unconditional love, I don't know where I would be. Thank you for never leaving or giving up on me, and thank you for using me to deliver this message.

Mom, I love you so much. Thank you for teaching me to be strong and to believe in the beauty of my dreams. Things were not always easy, but my siblings and I are who we are today because you raised us with your love. To the men I call Dad: You both have touched my life in such a special way and nothing can ever change that. Brandon, you are my brother and my friend. I am so thankful to have grown with you through the years. Shelbi' and Tyrani', my baby sisters, I love and believe in you both. Nanny, Madea, Pa Lawrence, and Pa Lou, you guys have been more than just grandparents; you have been wisdom, comfort, love and support. Thank you for everything.

The preparation of this book had the support of so many people. Tyrus and Jaime Thomas, you guys have the biggest hearts! Thank you for supporting and believing in my dream.

My dear friend Ana Storer, you are so talented. Thank you for pouring your heart into each painting in this book. Tony Gaskins Jr., Brandon White, Glen Davis, Britney Temple, Robert Chapman, Vann McCloud, and Mario Spann, thank you for providing answers to the questions every young athlete should know. Arlene W. Robinson, you are an awesome editor. Thank you for all of your hard work. To my wonderful attorney, Spencer Bowman, thank you for your patience and guidance throughout this process. Taiese Nevels, my fellow author, thank you for the long talks and many words of encouragement. Sevetri Wilson, there were so many times when I didn't know which way to go. Thank you for holding my hand and allowing God to use you. LaRanda Spann, words cannot express my gratitude towards you. Thank you for always being in my corner.

Jessica Gauthier, Barry Honore, Chris Davis, Brittney Dickson, Micah Hagen, Kortney Myles, Justin Romeo, LaShonda Freeman, Ashley Rodney, Urooj Sheikh, and Jessica Plummer: You all have helped me throughout this process in one way or another and I just want to say thank you.

Last but not least, Lawrence, you have been by my side for a long time. Thank you for listening to my thoughts and encouraging me to pursue my dreams. Most of all, thank you for believing in me even when I didn't believe in myself.

To my readers, thank you for your support and taking time to listen to what I have to say. ☺

FOREWORD

will [wil]

noun

power of choosing one's own actions: to have a strong or a weak will.

Will is what enabled a nauseated and profusely sweating Michael Jordan to fight through influenza in Game 5 of the 1997 NBA Finals. Not only did he fight, he scored 38 points and led his team to victory, ultimately a championship that year. Will is what allowed Nelson Mandela to remain strong and true to his beliefs while serving 27 years, of a life sentence, in prison. Will is what drove the both deaf and blind Helen Keller to earning a Bachelor of Arts degree. Will allowed Jackie Robinson and Bill Russell to break racial barriers in professional sports. If you obtain the will to carry on, you will never be defeated. Not saying you will not face adversity and obstacles, but you will never be defeated.

Will is what pushed me. Not being highly recruited out of high school, I had a strong desire to play basketball at a high level. My will got me there. Being asked to "walk on" by the university literally in my backyard could have crushed me. My will wouldn't let that happen. After later receiving a scholarship offer from them, I vowed to show them they made a mistake by initially not offering me a scholarship. It was my will that pushed me to help lead my team to the Final Four.

Will is in you whether you want it to be or not. It could be a weak will, or strong enough to enable you to carry on.

Tyrus Thomas
NBA Player / Philanthropist

INTRODUCTION

In three words I can sum up everything I have learned about life. It goes on.

~Robert Frost~

The first time I fell in love was the day I picked up a basketball. I was five years old and I thought that we would be together forever, but, little did I know the day would come when I would experience the biggest heartache as we parted ways and I had to live life without it.

When my athletic career came to a halt, I thought my whole world had ended. I felt frustrated and confused, because I was not ready to let go. In my mind I still had talent and in my heart I still had a dream. I had dismissed the notion that my ability to play sports was an opportunity to gain a few of the tools that would help me on my journey because, after fifteen years of echoing within this pattern, I had become acclimated to life as an athlete.

So, what happens when repetition meets change, and the thing that you are so accustomed to doing takes a different path from the one that you are treading? You trust God. It took some time but, by the grace of God, I came to understand that my path had turned, and if I wanted to meet success, I had to turn with it.

Though prayer and perseverance enabled me to carry on,

I noticed the sufferings of others who were striving to do the same. My inspiration for writing this book is to show young athletes that, in their times of disappointment, they are not defeated and they are not alone. There is someone out there who has experienced the same hardship and was able to find the will to persevere through the struggles of their distress. I want young athletes to understand that for each of the many stages they might diverge from in their pursuit to achieve their dreams, there is still a clear opportunity for success.

The following chapters tell real-life stories about the challenges and triumphs of six young athletes. The reader will understand a few of the many emotions these athletes endured and the tools that helped them overcome adversity and lead them past their disappointments. This book will provide a means of inspiration while ensuring that, when all is said and done, there is a life after sports. There are still games to be played, championships to be won, and challenges to be conquered. The transition might not be easy, but remember to trust God and understand that sometimes it takes a different kind of dream to make you smile.

Since we all have a different story and we all walk a different path, I want young athletes to know that the true measure of success is by what they do with the ability God has given to them. I hope that upon reading this book, you will find the same inspiration I did and understand that as your pages turn in life, you have the God-given ability to turn with them.

Love,
TaRhonda

CHAPTER 1:
YOUTHFUL THINKING

*Youth is easily deceived because it is
quick to hope and to imagine.*

~Aristotle~

When children see the life they want, they incur high hopes and big dreams. They then move gracefully through their childhood without any doubt in their minds that what they dream as a child will become their reality as an adult. Many children whose world revolves around sports proclaim their childhood dream as wanting to become a professional athlete, but statistics prove only a few will succeed past the cutoffs that will be implemented upon their horizons. For the children who do not make it, from grade school to college, how do they think and what do they feel when they realize their dream will not come true? Whatever their thoughts and feelings, I believe in spite of their disappointments they can still be successful if they have the will to carry on.

It was halftime in the second round of the 2003 Mississippi State Playoffs when the Tigers entered the locker room. Coach Henry looked at each player on his team and said, "We have come too far to just give it all away. If you guys don't pick up the pace, you'll lose and your season will be over." He then looked at his seniors and said, "This may very well be the last game of organized football many of you will ever play, so go out there and give it your all." With this in mind, each player entered the second half in a heap of passion. As a team, they battled and put up their best fight, but their efforts were not enough and in the end the game was lost. This unwanted defeat set the stage for a long ride home.

As the players loaded the buses, some in tears, many of them were greeted by family and friends who were waiting to acknowledge them for the end to a great season. Joshua, one of fifteen seniors on the team, embraced his mother with a warm hug before stepping onto the bus and walking to sit in his usual seat. As the bus slowly pulled away from Saga Stadium, he sat there sad and in awe, gazing out of his window at the place where it all so long ago began.

At the tender age of six, Joshua and a few of his teammates played their first football debut on a PeeWee team in the very same stadium. Back then, they were only kids, playing and idolizing professional athletes such as Deion Sanders and Emmitt Smith. At that time, they were not exposed to the seriousness of the game because in their youthful days there wasn't any. Football was purely fun, and so were any other sports they could play.

As Joshua made progress in the development of his athletic abilities, he proclaimed his childhood dream of wanting to become a professional athlete. In his declaration, he not only enjoyed the idea of doing something he loved, but also the idea of becoming famous and making millions. With the encouragement and influences of those around him, he believed one day his dream would come true.

As he sat on the bus, frail and cheerless, Joshua remembered his answers to different questions he was asked by people throughout his childhood.

What do you want to be when you grow up?

"A professional athlete," he would reply.

Who are your role models?

"Barry Sanders and Jerry Rice!"

Is school important to you?

"Yep! I'm going to Louisiana State University and play in Death Valley for Coach Gerry DiNardo, and then I'm going to the NFL!"

As many children do, Joshua devoted his heart and time to doing the one thing he became accustomed to and had grown to love. Even though witnessing the many dreadful disappointments of friends, former teammates, and other athletes enabled him to understand that his youthful dream might not happen, the possibility never really hit him until now.

Joshua was in his senior year of high school, exactly five months away from graduation, and he had not been recruited. The season had ended but he had not received any offers to attend college and play football. Saddened and disappointed, he felt confused because he spent the last eleven years of his life indulging in an atmosphere that enabled him to hope and dream of one day becoming who he wanted to become. *What am I going to do now?* he said to himself while sitting in his room, looking at all his accolades. *I don't want to do anything else. I have spent my whole life playing football and now they tell me I have to do something different. And college, I don't know how I'm gone pay for that!* Mentally, Joshua had never prepared for the

"Do well in high school in case you do not receive a scholarship."

~Robert Chapman

3

day he would have to move on and live life pursuing new dreams. Throughout his childhood he was always hopeful; never considering the question, *What if I don't make it?*

MOVING ON

After high school, Joshua was fortunate enough to attend an in-state institution under the assistance of financial aid. He decided that the disappointment of ending his football career would not define who he was as a young man. Upon entering college, it was not long before he realized the skills and talents he acquired as an athlete were not wasted, because they proved to be extremely beneficial in his college agendum. As a student, he remained competitive in his challenges by taking on the classroom as his arena and the curriculum as his opponent. As a leader, he willfully engaged in numerous professional and campus organizations; and because he was still an athlete at heart, he joined an intramural football team. The more engaged Joshua became in his environment and schoolwork, the more opportunities arose.

By declaring a career in medicine and seeking to develop himself as a young professional, he obtained several internships and attended a number of professional conferences. Through his traveling and networking experiences, he became exposed to a part of life he never knew existed. A young man from southern Mississippi, Joshua never realized there were so many other aspiring young professionals just like him. As he grew on his journey, he came to find a newfound respect for life as he had known it. He learned there was so much more to life than playing football, and that he could become successful in many aspects other than athletics.

ANALYSIS

In this real-life synopsis we explore the emotions of a kid whose dream of becoming a professional athlete came to a rest upon the end of his high school career. From childhood to young adulthood, Joshua completed a cycle of growth because he endured the process of having to deal with both the joys and disappointments of life. The irony in his story is that, as a child, he displayed the prevalent mindset of many children who participate in athletics, and the reality is that approximately one out of every one thousand (less than one percent) will live their dream of becoming a professional athlete. The rest must find a way to live life and carry on.

The moment Joshua faced at the end of his season during his senior year in high school is a pivotal moment in the lives of many young athletes when they are hit with the reality that their life's plan has taken a different path. After years of hoping, dreaming and compulsive repetition, many of them will do one of the following:

1. Earn an athletic scholarship that will enable them to continue to pursue their dream of becoming a professional athlete.

2. Not earn an athletic scholarship but attend college, at their own expense or on an academic scholarship, and continue to pursue their dream by earning a spot on a team as a walk-on.

3. Part ways with athletics, enter into college on an academic scholarship or financial aid, and focus on developing a career as a young professional.

4. They will not go to college at all.

Grade School: Every year, thousands of children between the age of five and thirteen are introduced to the world of athletics. Whether it's passing the basketball court and football field while walking home from school or playing outside at recess, the accessibility of sports for children in this age group is enormous. Some choose to engage in athletics because they offer a fun way to compete amongst their friends, while others engage because of an elder's influence. Whatever their skill sets and reasons for evolving into the games, most young athletes find discipline, structure, and a sense of purpose.

High School: Unlike grade school when the competition is innocent fun, high school is typically where the first cut is initiated. In this phase, only the athletes who possess astonishing potential will land a spot on one of the many freshmen, junior varsity or varsity teams. This system enables players within every talent calibration to have the opportunity to aggressively and competitively compete against other players with similar skill sets. As these aspiring young athletes progress and become more fine-tuned in their development, the talent pools become more intense because everyone wants to make it to the next level and scholarships are the most prominent way to get there. Nevertheless, approximately one out of every twenty-five (less than four percent) of these high school athletes will compete in collegiate sports.

College: As if you could not guess, there are only a handful of young athletes who will receive the opportunity to compete on the collegiate level. The ones who make it will either incur an extended four to five-year period to see their dream through or be forced to transition into life and become a productive citizen. For many aspiring young athletes, college is the final cut in the pursuit to becoming a professional athlete because only one out of every thirty (less than three percent) of collegiate athletes will have the opportunity to compete professionally.

AUTHOR'S NOTE

Often time, young athletes have a hard time adapting to change when they are called to tread a new path because many of them experience fear from a loss of structure, and from no longer being able to partake in the one thing that gave them hope and a sense of purpose. These athletes should know that their opportunity to become successful does not depend on their ability to play a sport or to become a professional athlete; rather, their future success depends on their ability to surmount their obstacles and never give up. We all have a dream, and we all wish it would come true, but the reality is that everything is not meant for everyone. That does not mean you cannot still be successful, it just means the path that you were taking was simply not a part of God's plan for your life.

There was a time when young athletes used their athletic abilities as collateral to earn a scholarship and complete their college education. If children could understand this concept then, when the time comes to move on, their hearts will be less hardened. The skills they obtain, such as discipline, dedication, and the ability to work hard, will be their guide and prove beneficial as they transition in life. Furthermore, they need to understand it is okay to analyze both sides of a possibility and to develop a backup plan; if Plan A does not work out, life will still go on and, to triumph, they must find a way to adapt. It is my experience that faith and preparation plays a big role in how we carry on and in whom we choose to become. When you know you have worked hard at your dreams and given them your best, just be at peace and accept what God allows.

REFLECTION JOURNAL

> ➢ Do you dream of becoming a professional athlete?

> ➢ Knowing the odds are against you, what is your plan for life after sports?

> ➢ Are you prepared to pursue that plan?

_____

_____

_____

_____

_____

_____

_____

_____

_____

_____

_____

_____

REFLECTION JOURNAL

_____

_____

_____

_____

_____

_____

_____

_____

_____

_____

_____

_____

_____

_____

REFLECTION JOURNAL

_____

_____

_____

_____

_____

_____

_____

_____

_____

_____

_____

_____

_____

_____

_____

_____

_____

REFLECTION JOURNAL

CHAPTER 2:
THE PARENT

*Sometimes, parents have to give up their
dream so their children can have one.*

~Unknown~

Have you ever known a young athlete whose main concern was to live up to the expectations of their parent: by playing a certain sport, producing boastful records, or even continuing a legacy by competing at a certain program? I have known many, and the consequence of such pressures can be quite damaging to these athletes' careers, hindering their thoughts, confidence and ability to naturally perform at their greatest potential. The parents of these athletes come in many different characters and affect their children in many different ways. The following story is just one example.

Stacie was a second year grad student when she began volunteering at a local high school as a motivational speaker. Young and full of passion, she was a former standout athlete who found joy in using her free time to share her experiences with other young athletes. One day during an after school mentor session that she was hosting, one of the kids asked her what she wanted to do when she was done with grad school, and how it related to her volunteering her time to athletic programs. Stacie said she was going to be a parent coach for the parents of young athletes; mainly nonprofit charity work, hosting informational workshops that will teach parents effective ways of supporting their children in sports and extracurricular activities. Someone else asked what was her motivation, and she began to tell a story about a girl she called Lena.

> Lena was in her sophomore year of high school when she was named the number-one outside hitter in the state of Texas. Since volleyball was one of the more competitive female sports, this meant that Lena was ranked among the best in the nation. Her mother Karla, who was responsible for much of Lena's training and premature success, was a well-known volleyball All-American who turned coach. Although Karla found much success in her coaching career and in helping young girls, she always dreamt of coaching Lena. But since the right opportunity never presented itself, Karla made it her priority to ensure that Lena remained at the top. This meant that she often played mom second to coach. Karla loved Lena but took pride in who she was as an athlete and had the potential to become.

PRE-GAME

Moments before their season opener, Lena and her teammates sat in the locker room as they mentally prepared for a match against their rival team. As she sat there, she engaged in a conversation with her teammate Rebecca, who played as the team's star defensive specialist. "Tonight is going to be a tough one," Lena said.

"Yeah, I feel like we have a bull's eye on our backs, Miss Number One," Rebecca replied and innocently laughed aloud. "Is your mom coming tonight?"

Lena glanced away, and with a blank stare, she replied, "Of course. When have you known my mother to ever miss a game? From as early as I can remember, she has never missed, not even one game."

"Man, Lena! It must be really nice to have such a strong support system," Rebecca said. "Throughout my career, my parents were hardly ever there because they were always working. I'd give anything to look in the stands and see my mother's face."

"Yeah, it has its ups and downs. I'm thankful my mother has always been there, but sometimes I just wish she didn't push so hard," Lena replied. "It's hard having a parent as a coach because sometimes they don't understand the importance of just being a parent."

"Yeah, I guess I never thought about that," Rebecca said.

"Time to play ladies! Let's warm up," interrupted their coach.

GAME TIME

When her team took the court, Lena knew she had to play her best game. She knew the crowd would be big and that her mother would be there front and center. Upon entering match four, Lena and her team were leading the series 2–1 after winning matches one and three 15–10 and 15–13. At the beginning of match four, Lena was up to serve. As she jumped up and pulled back, the ball soared over the net and out-of-bounds. "That's okay Lena. Let's go," yelled her teammates from the bench in a harmonic chant. Lena looked over to her mom while she got down for the next play. "Let's go Lena," yelled Karla as she stood to her feet.

As the game continued, Lena rotated to the left front position, where she was notorious for her forceful spiking. On the next play, the ball was set to Lena but when she went up to attempt the kill, the ball floated over the blockers and out-of-bounds. Frustrated and annoyed, she could not help but glance over at Karla, and watched her get up and walk out of the gym. Rebecca, who was subbing into the back row as the team prepared for defense, quickly approached Lena and said, "Hey! Pick your head up. We have a game to win and we need you." then she added, "You can do this Lena! Don't worry about your mom, come on!"

Although mentally Lena was unable to fully recover, with the encouragement of her teammates, she was able to play the role that needed to be played to help her team win.

After the game, she walked outside to find her mother waiting in the car. As she opened the door to step inside, Karla looked at her and said, "I don't know where your head is Lena, but I know you can play better than that. Your performance today was very unacceptable and I expect more. When you are Number One, there is no room for error. Do you understand me?"

Lena looked at her mother and said, "I'm sorry." Karla then drove away and they headed home in silence.

After telling the group this story, Stacie asked the students how many of them have or know someone who has a parent similar to what Lena had. Amazingly, more than half the children in the room raised their hands. She then asked if anyone could tell her what they thought happened to Lena in the end. Someone raised their hand and said, "She had a breakdown." Someone else yelled out, "No, she got tired of being intimidated and told her mom not to come to any more of her games." Everyone laughed aloud. Stacie chimed in and said, "No, not exactly. Let me tell you a little bit about Lena's ending."

GAME OVER

Karla's plan to ensure that her daughter was successful and remained on top came to pass. By the time Lena had reached her senior year of high school, she was one of the most heavily recruited freshmen in the country. She received scholarship offers from a number of college volleyball programs that hoped she would join their squad, but, under Karla's guidance, Lena chose to attend her mother's alma mater and continue a legacy.

Shortly after completing her freshman and sophomore years as a student athlete, Lena finally called it quits. Emotionally, she was drained, and playing volleyball just wasn't fun anymore.

The hardship of spending years of trying to live up to her mother's expectations eventually overpowered her love for a game that once brought her joy. The college experience of invariable comparisons between Lena and her mother helped her realize she had stopped playing for herself long ago.

Though the transition of parting ways with her life as an athlete was not easy, Lena found strength in knowing that her life had just begun. She utilized all the values that sustained her as an athlete while she sought to pursue a new dream, evolving into the classroom and developing her career as a young professional. Lena earned a bachelor's degree and is currently working on her master's degree. Stacie smiled and added, "Lena is me, and she is my motivation to help other young athletes and their parents."

> "Realize that God is just getting started with you. Sports have prepared you for LIFE."
>
> ~Britney Temple

ANALYSIS

Sometimes, parents don't understand the importance of just being a parent. This statement is perhaps one of the most powerful statements that can be made when it comes to parents and their children. The preceding story displays a prime example of a parent who lived her dream and then subjectively lived her daughter's dream as well. When dealing with young athletes, many parents fail to understand that the role they assume can be extremely detrimental in how their child responds in sports and in life.

Many athletes who endure the hardship of responding to their parents' elevated demands tend to incur a type of scorn and carry it throughout their future endeavors. As a result, some try harder with the notion that eventually they will surpass their parents' expectations, while others such as Lena just let go and find a way to carry on. There are several types of parents affiliated with sports and Karla represents only one. Let's look at a few more, and how their roles affect their children's lives.

The parent who is a lean supporter: Some parents have a profound understanding that it is the child who is undergoing the process of evolving as a young athlete. They recognize that the lessons and challenges their child is faced with will, in time, help him (or her) to be productive in life. These parents are natural in their ability to function solely as a support system, and place their child with a coach who has a genuine interest in developing young athletes. Most important, they encourage their child to pursue his (or her) own dreams while, as parents, they graciously step aside and watch him (or her) bloom.

> ➢ Young athletes who are placed in this circumstance do not necessarily have a better chance at success, but they do have a better opportunity to freely enjoy the sport they choose to play without the pressures and fears of not living up to their parents' expectations.

The parent who is anti-sports: For whatever reason, these parents are simply against the notion of their child competing in athletics. Some inherit a drawback—the memory of a failed aspiration or disappointment in their own career—while others feel the athletic world simply does not offer a realistic path to success. They feel the child will yield a greater chance of excelling in academics than in sports, and therefore neglect the basic tools that can be acquired and channeled throughout life. In their minds, they believe they are doing what is in the child's best interest, but in reality they are creating one of the biggest obstacles the child will have to strive to overcome.

> ➤ It can be extremely tough having a dream and wanting to pursue it but also having a parent who neither supports nor believes in what you seek to accomplish.

The parent who lives their dream through their child: Maybe they were not tall enough and did not make the cut. Maybe they did not receive the right exposure and publicity, or maybe it just was not their time. Whatever their reasons for attempting to live their dreams through their child, these parents can be extremely inconsiderate and overbearing. They create an undue stress that makes it hard for the child to connect with whom he or she desires to become as a person and has the potential to become as an athlete.

> ➤ Young athletes who endure the obstacle of fueling their parents' dreams tend to feel that their own dreams are not important.

The parent who is also a coach: These parents can be quite demanding, because they tend to hold high expectations. When given the opportunity to coach their child they tend to push extremely hard, expecting the child to step up and take a position of leadership. When not given the opportunity to coach their child, they tend to find a way to have a voice, which usually means coaching from the stands or behind closed doors. Consequently, when parents and coaches have different views, the child usually suffers. On one end is the coach who sets the pace for his team; on the other end is the parent with his own opinion of how things should be done.

> ➤ The effect these parents have on young athletes can

lead to a host of emotions and confusion. Imagine your coach telling you to "Run the plays," and then imagine your parent yelling from the stands, "Shoot the ball" or fussing all the way home about the shots you missed or did not take. Can you imagine?

The parent who antagonizes the coach: While some parents pressure the child, these parents pressure the coach. They believe the coach is the sole reason the child succeeds or fails. Whether they are taunting from the stands or behind closed doors in private meetings, these parents will do anything to see their child in the spotlight.

> ➤ The effect this parent has depends on the child's mindset. Some children are embarrassed by the agonizing ranting and raving of their parents, while others are totally fine with their parents lobbying their battle.

The parent who keeps a running tally of their child's stats: Some parents care about nothing except the numbers their child is able to produce. Have you ever seen a parent sitting in the stands with paper and a pen? They're easy to spot! Then there are the ones who quietly sit back and mentally keep track of every play. These parents create the type of environment that makes it impossible for their children to enjoy the sport.

> ➤ It is not uncommon for young athletes placed in this circumstance to neglect the importance of teamwork. While the team collectively works to defeat opponents, he (or she) is more focused on defeating "everyone" in the game.

The parent who is always working: Some parents are not able to be there the way they would like to because they must work to make ends meet. Other parents evolve into their jobs by choice and fail to realize the burden their absence creates.

> ➤ The athletes whose parents do what they have to do tend to understand that their parents are doing the best they can. The athletes whose parents do what they want to do tend to harbor resentment for all the moments they miss.

The parent who has wealth: Some parents believe their money can buy their child anywhere from a spot on the team to a position in the starting lineup. They are relentless in their ability to fund a tournament trip, pay for uniforms, or even make a "small" donation.

> ➤ Some athletes remain humble and work extra hard to prove they belong, while others become arrogant and accept the idea of their parents' money paving their way.

AUTHOR'S NOTE

Though we only discussed eight of the parent types, I am sure you can think of more. Each day, thousands of parents intuitively set high demands on their young athletes, failing to realize the pessimistic effects and overwhelming burdens they cause. The challenges these parents place before their children are a primary reason for resentment and broken relationships.

Young athletes need a support system and the freedom to unconsciously enjoy playing the sport of their choice. They need to know that it is okay if they are not the best player on the team or if they do not play for a certain program, because their parents will support and believe in them anyway. Most important, they should understand their ability to perform well in the classroom and obtain a good education is by far the most rewarding tool they can receive.

Although sports are a great way for children to gain the skill sets necessary to function in everyday life, it is not the only way to do so. Children need a balance. Summer camps, museums, community service, church organizations and youth conferences are all great tools that can help a child become well rounded.

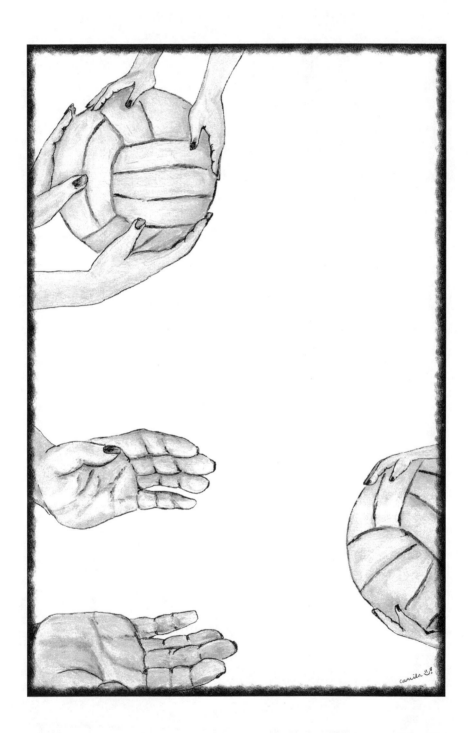

Reflection Journal

➤ Are you afraid of disappointing your parents based on your performance, decisions, or dreams?

➤ What do you wish you could communicate to them regarding the pressures you face?

➤ How will their support help lead you to success?

_____

_____

_____

_____

_____

_____

_____

_____

_____

_____

_____

REFLECTION JOURNAL

_____

_____

_____

_____

_____

_____

_____

_____

_____

_____

_____

_____

_____

_____

REFLECTION JOURNAL

REFLECTION JOURNAL

_____

_____

_____

_____

_____

_____

_____

_____

_____

_____

_____

_____

_____

_____

_____

CHAPTER 3:
THE COACH

*Coaching is fighting for the hearts and souls
of men and getting them to believe in you.*

~Eddie Robinson~

What fits the description of a good coach: an effective coach? Is it his ability to incur a winning season or boast of multiple championships? What about his ability to produce quality athletes and proclaim the best talent? The answer is none of the above. A strong leader is the epitome of what a good coach should be, because he is the heartbeat of whatever dynasty he is trying to fabricate. A good coach should be measured by the number of lives he touches and his ability to instill in his players the values that will inspire them to win not only in their sport, but also in life.

The 2001 Lagniappe Boys Basketball Championship was won by a team under the leadership of one of the most extraordinary high school coaches of all time. Coach Brinks took a team that no one thought could win and led them beyond the realm of success. He created an atmosphere that provided his team with the tools and mentality that drove them to exhale a perfect season of 36–0. The fact that this team stood an average height of five feet eight inches tall left many people asking questions such as, "How did they do it?" and "What helped them to get there?" Ironically, if you ask any player who was a member of this astonishing team, each one will tell a similar story of family, of passion, and of a coach who won the hearts and souls of his team while getting them to believe not only in him, but also in each other.

As we take a moment and look back through the eyes of one of the eleven players who shared in that victorious season, we gain a better understanding of what yielded the dynamics that led to the journey of one team's remarkable success.

"Discipline, hard work, and a lot of heart is what led us to the top! Coach Brinks was a big disciplinarian and he was someone who required a great deal of respect. He told us what he expected and never really presented us with any other options. Except the door! He led our team by giving us direction and by challenging us every day at practice. He always stressed the importance of team and because that's what we were, whenever any of us would make a mistake, we all paid the price. Most of the time, our grand punishment would be running. We would run anywhere from ten sixteen-second down-and-backs and then to half court, to two hours of strictly running until he would say stop.

For Coach Brinks, practice was like his battleground, because it was where he gave his players their stripes: mentally, emotionally, and physically, preparing us for any situation we might face. Therefore, when it was game time, he coached but never had to stress or say very much. See, we were all like brothers, so when the need was present, everyone had the green light to tell anyone what to do and, because we wanted to win, we would listen. I remember that year just like it was yesterday. As a team, I think we viewed the beginning of the season just as we did the end of it because we did nothing but play ball and work hard. We never even acknowledged the fact that we were undefeated until Coach Brinks talked about it, and by that time, we were already 26–0. Greed was never a threat to our team because, with the guidance of our coach, we all knew and understood our individual roles, and our franchise player was not proclaimed until the season was over and our championship was won. We trusted our coach.

It was easy to believe in Coach Brinks because he believed in us. In fact, he had the type of driven spirit that made everyone around him believe. With only one player on the team having been blessed to have his biological father in his life, our mothers viewed our coach as an away-from-home father, and they trusted that he had our best interest at heart. Playing for Coach Brinks was tough, because you had to be mentally strong and overcome the challenge of standing in your own way. When it was time to move on, not playing for Coach Brinks was even tougher, because there were very few coaches who took the time to set demands and develop the character of their players. Coach Brinks taught us about hard work and prepared us for life."

The recap of one coach's ability to take an underrated

team, who was as small in stature as this hearty group of young men, and build a legacy is only a fraction of what he was able to accomplish. Coach Brinks was more than just a coach. He was a teacher, a leader, a father, and (after graduation) a friend. He unconsciously prepared his players with the necessary tools for his athletes to win on the court as well as in their transitions in life. Aside from basketball, he ensured that his team developed a sense of purpose in the community by requiring they volunteered twenty hours each season toward helping others in ways that were invaluable. Coach Brinks also created a study system that monitored his players' grades and in-class performance. His mission was to ensure that even if players chose not to attend college, the opportunity to do so would be present.

This is not to say that every kid who ever played for him was saved from life's destructions, but—they were provided with the essential skill sets to make the right decisions and become successful. While the coach has an obligation to ensure that his players are well-rounded individuals, each player has the ultimate choice as to where his next stop will be.

ANALYSIS

At what point does a coach assume the responsibility of providing his players with the tools of success? He does so upon proclaiming his profession. The influence a coach has on a young athlete's life is so vital; he can never rid himself of his title. A coach takes on the burden of knowing the dreams and goals of his players, and because athletes remember everything, most of them will think of their coach in two thoughts: *He ruined my life* or *He changed my life*. Those opinions are not just built upon a coach's ability to help a kid become a professional athlete; they are built upon a coach's ability to prepare a kid for the challenges of life. Coaches should ensure that their players have

"There is life after sports so don't be afraid to move on!"

~Tony Gaskins Jr.

the grades that will provide them with the option of higher education. They should also teach the essence of discipline and respect, because those two attributes alone will allow countless opportunities. Some people will say there is a line between parenting and coaching, but the truth is, most young athletes spend a great deal of time in the presence of their coach, learning and developing skills that will help shape them into the person they will become.

When dealing with sports, a large number of the participants are young athletes who trust that the voice of their leader is worthy of believing in. This reason alone proves that everything coaches teach and expose have a momentous effect in the lives of their players. Let's discuss a few of the many factors that are important in coaching, and their roles among young athletes.

Coaching is a gift: The amazing thing about a gift is that, somewhere and somehow, we all have one. Among many factors that reveal a gifted coach is their natural ability to surface the full potential of each individual player. Another factor is their ability to be a viable student of the game, portraying the willingness to learn from various aspects, such as their players and fellow coaches, as well as victories and defeats. Since each player is different, a gifted coach has the willingness to understand the needs of his players and the things that will help them become successful.

Theoretically, today's coaching profession is flooded with a slew of former athletes who decided coaching would be the second best thing to playing; but just because you played the game does not mean you should coach the game. Since coaching is a gift, you either have it or you don't. And if you don't, then you must be careful; you are in danger of ruining the lives and athletic careers of many young athletes.

Winning and losing: Everyone wants to win! But when you are dealing with sports and young athletes, where does the winning truly begin? Is it with the titles and championships, or is it with the values and lessons that sustain them? Mark 8:36 says, "What good is it for a man to gain the world yet lose his soul?" Similarly speaking, what good is it for a kid to win thousands of games yet not be able to win in life? If coaches neglect to prepare their players with the essentials to complete a successful transition, then what has been won? The undeniable truth is when coaches fail to equip their athletes with the tools that will aid in life's journey; the number of games that are won becomes insignificant because, sometimes, when you win you really lose.

Attitude: It has been stated that your attitude, not your aptitude, will determine your altitude. In layman's terms, your talent alone will not suffice in your ability to achieve greatness, because your attitude ultimately determines the depth of your journey. When dealing with coaches and athletes, it is important for coaches to display the attitude they desire among their players, because attitude is one of the most contagious elements that can affect a group of individuals. As leaders, coaches have the responsibility of fueling a fire. And that fire should burn so bright; everyone around them cannot help but catch it too.

Team: The most notable phrase for this word is "Together Everyone Achieves More." One of the most beneficial teachings a coach can emphasize to ensure his squad is in unity with him and each other is the importance of team. Players should understand that together, as a unit, they win, and together they lose. To develop and maintain a healthy chemistry, each player should understand his or her role and responsibility. Some coaches make the mistake of playing their athletes against each other. They entice aggressive competition among their players as a way of challenging and motivating each player to work harder. This system works well for players who choose to use their coach's method as an incentive to become better and fight for a position. However, this system does not work well for players who feel outshone, or threatened as to their position or role on the team. They begin to view their teammates as their opponent, which causes a heap of turmoil and division.

Personal relationships: It is beyond important for coaches to procure a personal relationship with their players. Sometimes it is even helpful to go beyond the players and get to know where they come from. This allows coaches to understand their athletes as people and develop better approaches to help them meet success. A coach should not only be concerned with each player's talents and athletic abilities, but also with their thoughts, drives and ambitions. By portraying a genuine concern, coaches yield a better chance of gaining their players' trust for their leadership in the classroom, in sports, and in life.

AUTHOR'S NOTE

Coaches assume the most important role in the lives of young athletes because they serve as the primary leaders. They are responsible for molding young athletes with skills that will enable them to win, while focusing on the overall development of each individual player. Since their attitude and philosophy have the ability to affect their team's performance, it is important that coaches remain just in their teachings and expectations. Young athletes thrive best when they have structure and a clear understanding of the direction their coach is steering them in.

Coaches should serve as mentors, and allow their players to find comfort in being able to confide in them. When they take the time to motivate and encourage their players to give sincere efforts, coaches automatically provide the mental support young athletes need to believe in what they set out to achieve. Additionally, since coaches have the ability to build their players up, they should empower their players with the confidence and mindset to deal with the everyday challenges of life. Thus, when young athletes have completed their tenure in sports, they should possess the tools that will enable them to carry on as they strive to become successful in life.

Reflection Journal

➢ Have you had an influential coach in the course of your athletic career?

➢ How has that coach mentored or nurtured your dreams?

➢ What lessons or tools did they provide you with to carry through life's journey?

_____

_____

_____

_____

_____

_____

_____

_____

_____

_____

_____

REFLECTION JOURNAL

_____

_____

_____

_____

_____

_____

_____

_____

_____

_____

_____

_____

_____

_____

_____

_____

Reflection Journal

_____

_____

_____

_____

_____

_____

_____

_____

_____

_____

_____

_____

_____

_____

REFLECTION JOURNAL

_____

_____

_____

_____

_____

_____

_____

_____

_____

_____

_____

_____

_____

_____

_____

_____

CHAPTER 4:

THE CHOSEN ONE

*Talent is never enough. With few exceptions
the best players are the hardest workers.*

~Magic Johnson~

They say there is one in every thousand: the chosen one, the star, and that his talent is the reason he succeeds. But if they look past the surface, they will find that hard work is what really drives him to the pinnacle of his success. The difference between a talented athlete and a great athlete lies within the substance of his work ethic. A talented athlete has the natural abilities to play a sport, but a great athlete has the abilities plus the drive and ambition to go beyond the sport. To achieve greatness, it will take a lot more than talent to get there; it will take inevitable doses of desire and hard work. Let's talk about Tyler and his journey.

When Tyler entered high school, he was a scrawny little kid who had nothing more than a dream of playing basketball and a prayer to see it through. He was extremely talented and possessed a strong aptitude for the sport, but was challenged by the fact that his physical disposition was significantly smaller than the other athletes his age. Nevertheless, rather than allowing his size to steer him from his dream, he prayed for the confidence and abilities to push past his disadvantage.

During his freshman and sophomore years, Tyler participated as a member of the Panther Junior Varsity Basketball Team. His coach knew he was talented and believed that, in spite of his size, this position would allow him to thrive while developing his physical frame and becoming a stronger player. And it did. Apart from his team-related practices, Tyler took the initiative to work on his ball handling and shooting abilities. He also trained with an agility coach and completed twice the work required of him in the weight room. Tyler understood that if he wanted to stand out, he had to be the best, and that meant perfecting the fundamental components of his game. He trusted that if he took care of the possible, God would take care of the impossible. Furthermore, his work ethic helped him earn the respect from his teammates that allowed them to believe in his abilities as well.

Somewhere between the summer of his tenth and eleventh-grade year, Tyler must have eaten a magic beanstalk, because he endured a growth spurt that sprouted him from a height of five feet four inches to approximately six feet five inches. While others were in awe of his transformation, Tyler was just thankful to have finally received the size that complemented his abilities. In addition to his athleticism, his physique stimulated a buzz that qualified him as an NCAA Division One prospect and triggered a number of inquires and scholarship opportunities. Though he was heavily recruited by programs such as the University of Miami, Tyler chose to attend a university in his hometown because it gave him an unlimited amount of physical support from his family and friends. As he joined a team that was young and full of talent, Tyler was considered a solid addition because his leadership fueled a spark that inspired everyone in his midst.

When he began his freshman year, he was engulfed with a heap of expectations from everyone except his family and friends, who were just happy to see him living his dream. However, as they patiently waited, the day of his debut came to be longer than they had imagined.

During the preseason of his rookie year, Tyler suffered a neck injury that caused him to redshirt the entire season. Heartbroken and dismayed, his coaches remained optimistic about his return. They were sure that the challenges he endured throughout his career would enable him to persevere and overcome what seemed to be yet another obstacle. And without a doubt, they were right. After his medical release, Tyler worked to rebuild his strength and reap the most from his rehab. He trained with special coaches to regain the balance and muscle he needed to become strong again. Though his presence was missed on the court, he attended every practice, game, and study hall to show his team he was there in spirit.

When Tyler returned the next season, he did so with the goal of helping his team win an NCAA title. The previous season, he became a student of the game. He observed the strengths and weaknesses of his team and gained an understanding of what would lead them to success. He also came to understand the importance of his role, and how he could become a key contributor. When the season began, Tyler made his mark as he became known for his fearless shooting and shot-blocking techniques. Intermingled with his talent, his drive and ambition were the shadow behind his breakout season. Though his team did not win the NCAA title that season, he was able to help lead them to the Final Four Quarterfinal Championship.

The stats that Tyler put up that year were amazing, and were enough to put him on the radar as a prospect for the National Basketball Association. Needless to say, when he entered his name into the lottery pool, he was selected as a top-ten pick in the NBA draft.

ANALYSIS

In the discussion from Chapter 1, I stated that approximately one out of every one thousand young athletes who proclaim their childhood dream as wanting to become a professional athlete will receive such an opportunity. The preceding story portrays the journey of a young man who, through his work ethic and determination, was able to overcome adversity in every stage of his athletic career to live his dream and prevail as the chosen one. Tyler worked hard day in and day out to give himself the opportunity no one thought he would have. With every trial he endured, he became stronger in his ability to persevere.

"Become a star in your own life."

~Vann McCloud

Shortly after establishing his career in the NBA, Tyler began to recall the struggles he endured throughout his athletic career. As he reminisced, he thought about young athletes who might experience the same trials, and decided to develop a program to teach some of the tools that helped him on his journey. Let's evaluate the following principles and how you can capitalize them on your own journey.

1. **Character**: Talented athletes will work hard under supervised conditions, but great athletes will work hard when no one else is watching. It is important

for you to develop character, because it will provoke you to exercise integrity and discipline at all times. It will teach you to appreciate your wins and learn from your losses. It will teach you to have dignity and to understand that you could never cheat or get over on anyone else the way you could cheat or get over on yourself. Most important, it will teach you to take pride in who you are and in what you set out to accomplish while allowing you to not only become a great athlete, but also a great person. Your character will enable you to understand that the sport you play is more than just a game; it is also a teacher of life.

2. **Leadership**: When you have learned to be a humble follower, it is then that you will become a strong leader. Leadership will teach you to take initiative whenever the need is present, and entice you to continuously seek growth while motivating others to do the same. It will help you build a powerful brand that will allow you to gain the trust of both your coaches and teammates. Given that the role is not an easy task, everyone does not have the fortitude to withstand the responsibility. A great leader understands the true value of respect, honor, discipline and hard work. Leadership is perhaps the most important position a young athlete can assume throughout the course of his (or her) career. If you can manage to obtain such tool, then you will be well prepared for life.

3. **Work Ethic**: Young athletes should understand that greatness is more than just a state of mind,

because it takes an immense amount of work to get there and even more work to stay there. Developing a strong work ethic will enable you to understand that all the time and effort you put into becoming a better athlete will prepare you to reap many of life's most rewarding harvests. Some might be reaped immediately, while others might be done in the long term. Either way, since hard work is the root of success, it will always pay off.

4. Determination: When you possess the presence of determination in your soul, you will persevere through all of the challenges and hardships you are bound to encounter. Determination will enable you to become adamantly driven about everything you set out to accomplish, and push you to allow nothing to deter you from your dreams. When the road gets tough and you want to give up, determination will teach you to be patient. When you find that you are giving your best effort and it is still not enough, determination will help you to reload with the persistence that will allow you to endure.

5. Faith: It is important for you to maintain your faith through every case of adversity and disappointment. There will be many times when people will doubt you and tell you to just move on, but when you believe in who you are and aspire to become, nothing can stop you from getting to where you are going. In life, you will find that believing in yourself is the primary key to success, because if you don't believe, then no one else will. The Bible says that faith is the substance of things hoped for and the evidence of things not seen. When you find this kind of faith, you will learn to take care of what is possible and to trust God with what seems impossible.

AUTHOR'S NOTE

Many people might believe that the chosen one supersedes the other nine hundred and ninety-nine because of his talent, but I believe he succeeds as the result of a combination of his overall abilities. He is talented and confident, but humble and hardworking. He is the best because he takes pride in doing the work he knows will enable him to grow in his abilities and succeed. Each day he challenges himself, even in his darkest moments, because he understands the notion that hard work will outshine his talent when his talent is not willing to work hard.

In one light or another, everyone has the desire to achieve success but, in the same lights, not everyone is willing to put in the work it requires. Success requires you to remain focused in spite of your fears and disappointments. It requires the patience to be at peace and the faith to endure as you humbly await your opportunity to lead, contribute and shine. It requires you to accept criticism and rejection, yet trains you to persevere and never give up. And because of the journey you must take to get there, success will teach you to appreciate where you come from and look forward to where you are going.

As you travel the road to success, you should know it is not a straight path. It can be lonely and dark with many curves, wrong turns and unforeseen obstacles. Even more frightening, it is free of any roadmaps as each individual must find their own way. But be encouraged and know that you can make it!

CHAMPION

REFLECTION JOURNAL

- ➤ Do you give one hundred percent each time you play the sport you love?

- ➤ How will your work ethic impact who you become?

- ➤ What sacrifices will you make to reach your full potential?

_____

_____

_____

_____

_____

_____

_____

_____

_____

_____

_____

_____

REFLECTION JOURNAL

_____

_____

_____

_____

_____

_____

_____

_____

_____

_____

_____

_____

_____

_____

_____

_____

REFLECTION JOURNAL

_____

_____

_____

_____

_____

_____

_____

_____

_____

_____

_____

_____

_____

_____

_____

_____

_____

_____

REFLECTION JOURNAL

CHAPTER 5:
THE GAMBLER

*A man cannot discover new oceans unless he
has the courage to lose sight of the shore.*

~Andre Gide~

What time is the right time to step out on faith and chase after your dreams? Tough question, right? That's because there is no correct answer. We all have a different rhythm and we move according to the beats our hearts crave. Some choose to listen to the tone as they await the right moment to join in, while others choose to dance without fear every time their beats drop. In a life that is full of uncertainties, the most difficult decisions involve the greatest amount of risk. I believe every young athlete faces a point in their careers when they must choose between their hearts and the status quo. The following story yields a perfect example.

When Charlie quit school, it was at the end of his basketball season during his senior year of college and he had one thing on his mind: "Going pro!" Unlike many of the traditional student athletes, who viewed sports as an opportunity to receive an education, Charlie viewed education as an opportunity that would help him to play basketball. Throughout his high school and college career, he never showed a genuine interest in his studies. He attended all his classroom and study hall sessions but did just enough work to maintain his eligibility. Day in and day out, the only thing he thought about was what it would be like to one day live the reality of his dream.

Months before making his decision, Charlie confided in his father, the one person he trusted and admired most, "How would you feel if I quit school for now to go play basketball?"

His father looked at him and said, "No son, how would you feel if you quit school to go and play basketball?"

Charlie gripped the ball that he was holding, and then said, "Honestly Pop, I would feel like I was doing what my heart needed me to do. I mean, right now, I go to school every day but my mind and heart isn't there. I feel like if I don't take this chance, I'll spend the rest of my life wondering what could have happened. And I don't want to live like that."

Charlie's father took the ball out of his hands and said, "Have you thought about the possible consequences of your actions … I mean, if you don't make it?"

"Yes sir, I have," Charlie replied.

"And this is what your heart wants huh?"

"Yeah, it is," Charlie said.

"I've raised you son. And I would never stand in the way of your dreams. If this is what you want, then follow your heart."

His father's approval gave Charlie the peace he needed as he set out to pursue a career as a professional basketball player. And though he only needed three classes to complete his undergraduate degree, he did not think twice about his decision because he felt he could always go back to school. He knew his journey would not be easy, but in his heart he believed that, if he put in the work and made the right connections, he could make it.

Just as Charlie began to search for a manager, he received an unforeseen phone call from a credible agent who worked with several big-name players. The agent explained that he had received some game footage along with a strong recommendation on Charlie's behalf and was interested in representing him. After taking a brief moment to exhale, Charlie accepted the offer and was beyond thankful. From that moment on, things seemed to be heading in the right direction.

Upon connecting with the agent, Charlie began working with personal and nutritional trainers to get his body in tip-top shape. After three months of hard work, his coach was able pull a few strings to get Charlie a tryout for an NBA professional summer league team. When he first heard the news, he was excited because he felt he was finally getting the opportunity he had long awaited. But then when he stepped into the arena, reality set in and his feelings began to change.

Charlie was one out of eighteen prospects vying for a position and, because he had come from a smaller university, he was the only small-name player. While he put forth stellar performances during workouts, he could not help but observe the behind-the-scene politics and realized that his chances of a successful outcome would be slim to none. And he was right. Four days into the tryout, Charlie was cut. Though disappointed, he did not let that deter him from chasing his dream.

He spent the next few months working on his game while his agent was busy trying to find him another opportunity. But as time began to wind down and jobs became scarce, his agent decided they should consider a different path: "At this point I think we should explore options other than the NBA. Time is passing, and the competition is really stiff. If you want a real shot, I think we should pursue the D-League. It's a step below the NBA but a good way to get your name out there. There are sixteen teams and ten players on each team. If this doesn't work, then the next step will be overseas. What do you think?"

"I think I'm willing to do whatever it takes," Charlie replied.

Charlie spent the next two years competing in the D-League before he was picked up by a professional basketball team overseas. Although he did not receive an opportunity to play in the NBA, he was satisfied with his efforts and the choices he had made. After three years of playing overseas, he decided he was ready to go back to school and complete his education. Since he had followed his heart and experienced what he felt he needed to experience, Charlie was more focused and better prepared to do what he knew he needed to do.

ANALYSIS

The preceding story is not to infer that young athletes should quit school, but to demonstrate that they should never be afraid to step out on faith. Charlie came to a crossroad at the end of his collegiate career when he was faced with what many people

"Don't lose sight of your dream because someone thinks you can't do it."

~Glen "Big Baby" Davis

would view as a life-changing decision. Though society expected him to complete his education and begin to pursue a career as a working professional, Charlie chose to follow his heart and pursue his dreams as a professional athlete. The support he received from his father coupled with the faith he had in himself and in his dream gave him the strength he needed to overlook his mental fears and give his heart a chance.

Upon the end of their careers, few young athletes possess the substance to listen to their hearts and fulfill their personal cravings; they allow their fears and life's status quo to take the lead. Of the many who do not listen, some will move on and meet success just fine, while others will one day wake up and experience a heap of regret. Of the few who do listen, many will achieve the ultimate goal of finding peace of mind, while others will lose sight of the goal and become trapped within their dream.

There are several avenues young athletes should consider when they are in the position to make decisions that will affect the rest of their life. Regardless of what they choose to do, it is important that these young athletes do what they want to do. Let's take a look at a few of these factors and how the concept of understanding each area can be of great benefit, and help sustain you as you learn to make decisions for your life.

Mind versus Heart: There will be many times in your life when your mind and heart will be at war. Your mind will tell you to do one thing and your heart will tell you to do something different. In those moments you must understand the importance of choosing the path that has your heart in it, because it is then that you are more likely to reach your full potential. Though it might seem safe to listen to your mind, it can be unwise if you allow it to stop your heart from beating. On the same note, win or lose, once you have given your heart a chance, you have to know when to move on.

Decision Making: They say that sports are twenty percent physical and eighty percent mental because every challenge requires the cerebral toughness and ability to think even in the most adverse circumstances. You must understand that you are your biggest opponent, and that if you lose mentally, you will lose everything. When you are physically tired and feel like you want to quit or give up, you must allow your mental ability to push you past your pessimism. The decisions you make throughout your career are important because, big or small, they will have altering affects on your life. Whether it's having the courage to take the game-winning shot, studying all night to ace an important exam, or choosing to go against the status quo and chase after your dreams, the two most important things you can learn as a young athlete is the reward of sacrifice and the dynamics of being able to make a decision and live with it.

Risk: One can infer that the life we live can be defined by the types of risk we are willing to take. The experience of taking risks can enable you to grow, because it will release you from the fears that hold you back. Since the results can be either positive or negative, you must be prepared to deal with every consequence that could occur. Taking risks will help you develop the necessary confidence to supersede any obstacles that might lie within your path. The process can also provide you with the tools that will enable you to improve on your weakness while giving you the courage and peace of tempting the unknown. As a young athlete, you should understand that every great success story involves taking risk.

Fear: They say to find the thing that scares you most and run toward it, but often time we run away from it due to the fear of failure and disappointment. It is not wise to view every fear in a negative light, because your reservations could keep you from achieving your dreams. Be fearless with your aspirations and trust that you are capable of tapping into abilities that will enable you to grow. If you are always afraid to step out on faith, opportunity will pass you by and you will never dicover the life that is full of endless possibilities.

Happiness: Living to please other people is a great way to live miserable because, other than the fact that it is impossible please eveyone, you neglect the importance of pleasing yourself. True happiness comes from within, and depends on your desires and state of mind. To find it, you must seek to discover the talent God has bestowed upon you and not only do it, but do it well. Don't sacrifice your joy because you want to play it safe or please someone else. Remember, even if you fall, as long as you get back up, you will find happiness because you will have the peace of mind from doing what "you" wanted to do.

AUTHOR'S NOTE

Each year, thousands of young athletes face the decision as to whether they should move on and breathe out a new dream, or continue striving to birth the dreams they have been nurturing with the hopes of receiving their breakthrough opportunity. When you face tough decisions, it is easy to get trapped into doing what others feel you should do instead of doing what you want to do, but a major part of growing up is learning to make your own decisions. When you choose to listen to your heart and chase after your dreams you will experience many letdowns and disappointments, but you must remain strong. Even if you do not receive the opportunity to live your dream, you will still be able to carry on knowing that you tried and gave it your best shot.

There are several young athletes who had the potential to become something great but, for whatever reasons, did not go after their dreams. Consequently, some of them will live the rest of their lives thinking of the person they could have become and the amazing things they could have done. By the blessings of God, you control your destiny. Therefore, when you are pressured to make decisions that will affect your life, remember these words: "My Life, My Choice." It is important to understand that if you do what you want to do, you will do it out of love and the results will show. Life is short, but it can be extremely long when you are living to please others or doing something you have no desire to do. To be successful and happy, you should know why you are doing what you do, and you must do it for you.

REFLECTION JOURNAL

➢ What goal would you attempt if failure was not an option?

➢ Who or what is stopping you from achieving this goal?

➢ What will you do to move past the things that hold you back?

_____

_____

_____

_____

_____

_____

_____

_____

_____

_____

_____

REFLECTION JOURNAL

_____

_____

_____

_____

_____

_____

_____

_____

_____

_____

_____

_____

_____

_____

_____

_____

_____

_____

REFLECTION JOURNAL

_____

_____

_____

_____

_____

_____

_____

_____

_____

_____

_____

_____

_____

_____

_____

REFLECTION JOURNAL

_____

_____

_____

_____

_____

_____

_____

_____

_____

_____

_____

_____

_____

_____

_____

_____

_____

CHAPTER 6:
THE FINISHER

A gem cannot be polished without friction,
nor can a man be perfected without trials.

~Chinese Proverb~

It has been said that anything worth having does not come easy. My notion is experience and observation has proven this statement true. I believe many of the challenges young athletes face are mere elements set in place to help shape and build their character. I also believe if they endure their trials they will triumph, becoming more fine-tuned in their abilities and better prepared for life. In the discussion from Chapter 1, I mentioned the kid who does not get the scholarship, yet goes to college at his own expense and continues to pursue his dream by earning a spot on the team as a walk-on. The following story talks about a young man who lived the reality of this situation and the blessings of his triumph.

When Avery was ten years old, his mother said to him, "What do you want to be when you grow up?"

Avery grinned and said to his mother, "When I grow up, I want to be a basketball player and I'm gonna be the best one in the world."

Looking into his eyes as she knelt to hold his hand, his

mother then said to him, "Son, if you work really hard and never give up, you can be anything you want to be. The only thing I want you to do is to promise me you will go to college and get an education."

"Yes ma'am, I promise," Avery said to his mother.

Eight years later, as he prepared to enter into his freshman year of college, Avery still remembered the promise he had made to his mother and as he prepared to honor his word he did so without the assistance of a basketball scholarship. See, although Avery was one of the more talented players in his senior class, he grew up in a small town in Arkansas and was not recruited due to a lack of publicity and exposure. Nevertheless, because he still wanted to pursue his dream, he decided that in the midst of getting an education he would earn a spot on the UAPB Men's Basketball Team as a walk-on.

When the semester began, Avery made it a point to become acquainted with the members of the team. Since the season had not officially started, the players often engaged in open-gym pickup games, and Avery was at every session. One day as he was passing the athletic department on his way to class, he was stopped by one of the graduate assistants, who said, "Hey, your name is Avery right?" Avery replied, "Yes, I'm Avery."

Reaching his hand out to greet him, the assistant then said, "I'm Jason. I stopped you because I want you to know that I see your consistency in coming around the gym, and it seems as if you really want to become a member of the team."

Avery shook his head in agreement, saying, "I do, I really do!"

Then Jason said, "Where are you from?"

"Carthage," Avery replied.

"Carthage huh?" Jason repeated. "Okay. Well, this is what

I want you to do. Get me a highlight tape and some good game footage. If I like what I see, I'll do my best to help you get a tryout."

Without hesitation, Avery said, "Thank you. I really appreciate it. I will have it for you first thing tomorrow morning."

When Jason received the tapes, he did just as he said. He and one of the other assistants reviewed the footage, and both agreed Avery would be an asset to the program. Then they delivered the tapes along with their evaluations to members of the coaching staff, and within a week, Avery was called in for a three-day tryout. When he received the call, he was elated to finally get the opportunity he had been hoping for.

On day one of the tryouts, Avery performed a series of skill tests that allowed him the opportunity to showcase his individual ball handling and shooting capabilities. On day two, he scrimmaged with the team during their daily open-gym pickup games while the coaches looked on, observing his disposition as well as his ability to communicate and contribute in a team environment. Finally, on day three, he was called in for a one-on-one meeting with the head coach, Coach Frank.

In the meeting, Coach Frank broke the ice by saying, "Well young man, I am sure the last couple of days have been a little tough for you, playing and showcasing on a solo venture and all."

Avery smiled and said, "Yes and no. I just really want the opportunity to play for your program, so if that means stepping out on a limb, I'm willing to take that step."

Picking up the mini stress ball that was sitting on the corner of his desk, Coach Frank said, "Before I go any further, tell me, what is your motivation, and why should I give you a spot on this team?"

Without hesitation, Avery looked at Coach Frank and said, "Ever since I was a kid, all I wanted to do was play basketball, and in every stage of my career, I had a dream. When I was a kid, I dreamed of playing high school ball, and now that that's over, I dream of playing college ball. I know I have the ability to do great things, and if given the opportunity, I know I will be a great asset to your program."

Coach Frank then gave Avery his thoughts on what he and his staff had concluded about Avery's overall abilities throughout the tryout. "Well kid, I must say we are very impressed with your skills. You handle and shoot the ball very well."

"Thank you sir," Avery replied.

Continuing with his thoughts, Coach Frank then said, "We have a full twelve-man roster but because of the drive and ambition I see in you, in addition to your skill set, I am going to give you a shot."

Avery's heart skipped a beat. "Thank you Coach. Thank you so much!"

Coach Frank then said, "But! You should know that it won't be easy. You're a walk-on, which means you have to work ten times as hard. Are you prepared to do that?"

"Yes sir, I am," Avery replied.

Rising to his feet, Coach Frank reached over to shake Avery's hand, saying, "Welcome to the team."

Avery's commitment as a walk-on meant he would not receive the same financial privileges as every other member on the team. No scholarship, no book vouchers, and no housing or living expenses. In his mind, this challenge would only be temporary, and it was okay because he thought of it as the price he had to pay to achieve his mission. In figuring out a way to make it work, he lived at home and, in his off seasons, he engaged in a part-time job to pay his tuition and meet other needs.

Every season for the next three years, Avery continued the routine of working hard in the classroom and on the court, with the hopes of not only earning a starting position, but also receiving a scholarship. However, each season, while keeping him on the team, Coach Frank recruited around him, consistently bringing in other players. Physically and emotionally, Avery's dream had begun to take a toll on him, but he found inspiration in the fact that he was doing what he always wanted to do. In the times he wanted to give up and quit, he would pray and ask God for the strength to keep going. He would think of all the work he had put in, and truly believed his time would come; he just had to be patient. He also knew that while undergoing this process, he had to eliminate all negative voices that were telling him to just move on. His mother was his support system, because she was there through it all.

Finally, after finding himself engrossed with a fairly young team, Coach Frank looked to Avery, who was one of two seniors, as a veteran, and awarded him a full scholarship. Upon receiving his good news, Avery immediately went home to share it with his mother. "Momma! Guess what?"

Removing the spoon from the pot she was stirring, his mother replied, "What Avery, what's all the excitement about?"

Avery then said, "I got it, Ma. He finally gave me a scholarship."

As her eyes began to tear, his mother looked at him with the warmest smile and said, "No baby, he finally gave you what you deserve. I'm proud of you, Avery. I remember when you were just a boy and you promised me that no matter what happened, you would get an education. And you did. In four months, you will be graduating from college, and you are finally getting what you've worked so hard for. There were times when I wasn't sure if, as a mother, I should have stepped in, so I just prayed. And every time I felt you were safe, because what didn't kill you would make you stronger. Guess I was right. I watched you grow into a man, and I am so proud to be your mother. I know it wasn't easy, and it didn't come the way you wanted it to, but you did it. You earned it and it's yours."

Embracing his mother with a hug, Avery wiped her tears and said, "Thank you Mama … I love you."

ANALYSIS

While honoring his word to his mother, Avery was able to turn his dream into reality by overcoming his adversities. In the midst of his final season, he graduated with his bachelor's degree and was able to immediately begin graduate school. Shortly after the season ended, and he began to ponder the idea of pursuing a basketball career overseas, Avery was presented with the opportunity to complete his master's degree while working with the men's basketball team as a graduate assistant. When he considered the longevity of his options, Avery decided that accepting the graduate position would be of more benefit, since he could earn a free education and gain exposure in the profession that would help him to one day prevail as a college coach.

Perseverance enabled Avery to accomplish much more than he had set out to achieve because his determination pushed him to not allow anything to hold him back. Many young athletes who attempt to accomplish the task of joining a collegiate team as a walk-on fail to complete their mission because of the humility and hard work required. They give up

> "Don't ever give up! There is always something positive to gain from every negative situation."
>
> ~Brandon White

on their dream before it begins and never reap the bliss that awaits them at the end of their trial. Let's look at some of the tools that can help keep you grounded if you find yourself in such a situation.

1. **Education**: The thing about sports is that they are here today and gone tomorrow. Whether it's a torn ligament, a revoked scholarship, or a lack of publicity, sports can be taken away at any time, but an education is forever. Education is important because it will enable you to become a well-rounded individual. There is no better feeling than one of knowing you have earned something that NO ONE can take from you. Although you might have a dream of competing as a professional athlete, you do not know which curveball life will throw your way. Therefore, obtaining an education can be beneficial in having something positive to fall back on. Many of the young athletes who neither make it to the pros nor complete their education fall victim to the destructions of life, because once they dismiss the window of opportunity, they never find their way back to it. An education is by far one of the best tools any young athlete can acquire.

2. **Courage**: As you set out to achieve your dreams,

you will find that courage will enable you to face your challenges without fear, because it will push you to chase the dreams that seem far and out of reach. It will allow you to compete in front of large crowds when you are nervous or unsure, and teach you to try again when you make a mistake or experience disappointments. When no one else is willing to step up and be a leader, courage will enable you to be the example. Most important, it will help you cope with the daily rigors of being an athlete by giving you strength to overcome the many phases of adversity you will face throughout the course of your career.

3. **Hard Work**: If ever you find yourself wondering whether hard work pays off, tell yourself that, one way or another, you will always get out whatever you put in. Hard work will give you the confidence you need to perform at your greatest potential, and will allow you to overcome any barriers of doubt others might place before you. It will prepare you to deal not only with the physical challenges your body will encounter, but the mental and emotional challenges as well. Hard work requires a great deal of dedication and endurance and though the process might not be easy, the results will certainly be worth it.

4. **Perseverance**: If you persevere through your hardships, you will move to a higher level of achievement. There are many times when you will want to quit because you might feel the odds are against you, but do not allow your circumstances

to affect your ability to overcome your obstacles. Perseverance will enable you to have the strength to not give up when the road gets tough. It will allow you to push through your disappointments such as unforeseen injuries or limited playing time. Things might not happen the way you imagined them to, but if you persevere, you will see them happen the way God planned them.

5. **Humility**: A young athlete who practices humility is one who has found a path to success. Humility will enable you to master the mental strength you will need to deal with your coaches, teammates, opponents and everyday challenges in life. To be humble does not mean you are weak or shameful. It simply means you understand the notion that remaining modest through your trials and triumphs will enable you to continuously grow and set positive examples for those who are watching.

AUTHOR'S NOTE

It's amazing how the trials you endure as a young athlete can enable you to evolve a step closer toward becoming the person God created you to be. The obstacles you overcome are tests that will build your character and teach you to understand that when you have the drive to achieve your dreams, you will always emerge with profitable results. Though the process will not be easy, your faith will allow you to convert your stumbling blocks into stepping-stones, and perseverance will enable you to climb to a successful finish.

If you want something, you must work for it and understand

that no one else can make it happen but you. You must also understand that the challenges you will encounter are only there to make you stronger and, to prevail, quitting is not an option. Sometimes your dream might seem cloudy and full of rain but if you weather the storm, you will gain more than what you set out to accomplish. You will become more polished in your abilities and mentally prepared to face your next challenge. To compete as a young athlete is not an easy task, but if you work hard and think positive, you will find it is not impossible.

Reflection Journal

> ➤ Which characteristics do you possess that will keep you from giving up on your dreams?

> ➤ Can you remember a time when you used these qualities to overcome adversity?

> ➤ What did your experience teach you about your ability to persevere?

_____

_____

_____

_____

_____

_____

_____

_____

_____

_____

_____

_____

REFLECTION JOURNAL

_____

_____

_____

_____

_____

_____

_____

_____

_____

_____

_____

_____

_____

_____

_____

REFLECTION JOURNAL

REFLECTION JOURNAL

_____

_____

_____

_____

_____

_____

_____

_____

_____

_____

_____

_____

_____

_____

_____

_____

CHAPTER 7:

THE ANSWERS YOU SHOULD KNOW

Dreams are today's answers to
tomorrow's questions.

~Edgar Cayce~

Life is a journey, and we must travel until we get to where God wants us to be. The problem is, there are times when we become distracted by the place we feel we are supposed to be and fall so deep, it becomes impossible to believe we are capable of moving on. When we close one chapter in our lives, we must not dwell on the possibility of what could have happened. Instead, we must pick up our hearts along with our pride and trust that everything happens for a reason.

"I wasn't truly happy because I wasn't chasing after what God had for me."

~Marion Spann

Whether things transpire the way we want them to or not, we must understand that God is writing our story and, to receive the full extent of His blessings, each chapter must come to an end. We must learn to embrace every beginning with an open mind, and use our past trials and triumphs as the basis of our future inspiration.

Furthermore, as we press forward, we must help others by sharing our knowledge and experiences, just as the following individuals have chosen to share with you.

(The preceding stories are not related to the following individuals.)

Tony Gaskins Jr.

Author / Motivational Speaker / Screen Writer / Producer

Q: Today you are an author, motivational speaker and entrepreneur. How did you know when it was time to move on from your career as an athlete and what tools did you use to help in your transition?

A: "I was 21 when I gave up sports. After a series of injuries and bad relationships with coaches I came to the realization that there had to be something else out there for me. So I turned to writing, which is a gift I always had but ignored because I wanted to be a successful Pro Athlete."

Q: As you evaluate the success of your professional career and the time you spent as an athlete are you satisfied with the decisions you have made?

A: "I am satisfied because what I do now has just as much value as being and athlete with influence. Now I don't have to worry about wear and tear, wins and losses, and disappointments. I'm able to impact lives on a daily basis. I appreciate what sports did for me though. I learned a lot! I learned about hard work and perseverance. I carry that tenacious attitude into the work force now and it has benefited me greatly!"

Q: What is your advice to young athletes who are afraid to move on?

A: "Always know that there are other things you can do. Know that sports are not who you are but what you do! Identify your gifts, identify a career, make a plan and take action! If you can play sports then you can do anything! There is life after sports so don't be afraid to move on!"

BRANDON WHITE

TEACHER / COACH / GRADUATE STUDENT

Q: When you did not receive an athletic scholarship to compete on the colligate level you made the decision to tryout for a position as a walk-on. What is the biggest challenge that you encountered?

A: "In the beginning I endured the challenge of not receiving any playing time. I was always the last person to get on the court when my team scrimmaged. I remember standing on the sideline for the majority of practice, until the last five or ten minutes, before my coach would decide to sub me in with the rest of the guys. It was definitely a hard and humbling experience but I continued to work hard and refused to give up. As a result, by the end of my freshman year, I earned a position in the starting line up."

Q: I am sure there were times when you wanted to give up, but you didn't quit. What motivated you to persevere and keep trying?

A: "I didn't give up because I am not a quitter. I would never give up on anything. The process was hard but I always wanted to play college basketball, and when I received the opportunity there was no way I was going to allow anything to stop me from seeing it through. There were so many people who doubted me and told me to just move on, but I needed to prove them wrong and I needed to prove to myself that I could make it. It was all surreal"

Q: What advice would you give young athletes who might contemplate giving up in the midst of their trial?

A: "Don't ever give up! There is always something positive to gain from every negative situation. You have to keep your composure and not allow your challenges to get the best of you because giving up on the court will make it that much easier to give up in life. Remember, even if things don't work out in your favor, you will find pride in being able to look in the mirror and say, "I am not a quitter." I am a witness that Prayer + Hard Work = Success. Give it a try."

GLEN "BIG BABY" DAVIS
NBA PLAYER / PHILANTHROPIST

Q: How did your childhood experiences impact your goal of becoming successful?

A: "Everything that happened to me when I was younger shaped me into the man I am today. The good, the bad, the ugly...everything. As a result of my mother's drug addiction, I was forced to live with a lot of different families. It was from these relationships that I learned what I wanted for my future. I worked hard every day to make sure I didn't end up a statistic like everyone else around me. Who knows, maybe I wouldn't be as strong and driven and focused as I am now if it weren't for my childhood experiences."

Q: Though people often spoke of your potential to become a football star, you followed your heart and focused on your career as a basketball player. How did you cope with the pressures of people who tried to steer you away from your dreams?

A: "Everyone did their best to steer me away from playing basketball. "You're too fat", "you're too short", "you'll never make it", they would say. Although it did bother me to constantly hear those things, I could not and did not let it affect me. Instead, I used it in a positive way to motivate me to become the best basketball player I could be. I may have been ranked 25th in the country my junior year as a football player, but since childhood I dreamed of becoming a professional basketball player and would not let anything deter me from my destiny! Basketball was the love of my life, so it was easy for me to block out what everyone was telling me."

Q: What is your advice to young athletes who are faced with this dilemma?

A: "Visualization is the key. You need to be able to visualize yourself doing whatever it is you dream about. I visualized myself becoming a MacDonald's All American every day of my life until it happened. I thought about it so much it became an obsession of mine. Nothing could stop me. Don't loose sight of your dream because someone thinks you can't do it. The journey will be difficult but keep pushing. I think half the battle is believing in yourself and seeing yourself in that position. The rest is hard work. You have to be mentally tough to ignore the haters and disciplined enough to put in the hard work."

Q: You were drafted to the pros during your junior year of college. Do you ever consider completing your bachelor's degree?

A: "Yes, I do intend on completing my bachelors degree. I believe having an education is extremely important, especially when thinking about life after basketball. I am not just a basketball player. Did you know I was a drama major in college and have dreams of becoming the next Tyler Perry?"

"I also think having your degree is vital because it is something that you earned and no one can take away from you. Walking across that stage, shaking the school presidents hand and receiving your diploma is something that will always be yours."

ROBERT C. CHAPMAN
LAW ATTORNEY

Q: Many young athletes participate in sports with the dream of becoming a professional athlete, but you did so with the goal of becoming an attorney. How did you use your athletic abilities to fulfill your educational and personal goals?

A: "Becoming an attorney has always been my life long dream. I started playing football in high school because it looked like fun. Initially, obtaining an athletic scholarship wasn't anywhere on my mind because I was certain that I would receive some sort of financial assistance due to my academic achievements. However, as I approached the end of my senior year of high school, I received offers for partial academic scholarships and full athletic scholarships. It was at that point when realized I could get a free college education as a result of my athletic abilities and that became my incentive to perform well on the football field."

Q: During the years you spent training and competing as a student athlete what gave you the drive to not lose sight of your end goal?

A: "I always knew that playing football was just a means to an end. One thing that a lot of athletes ignore is the fact that there is going to be life after sports... I never lost sight of that. Football would only do so much; the rest was up to me. I knew that I would eventually have to take a different turn in life so I always kept becoming an attorney in the forefront of my mind."

Q: What advice would you give young athletes in regards to using their talents to achieve an education?

A: "The only way to obtain a higher education by using your physical talents is to receive an athletic scholarship to finance your education. However, don't depend on your talents to pay for school. Do well in high school in case you do not receive a scholarship. If you happen to possess the talent to receive a scholarship and do, then use it to the fullest. Get a free education!"

BRITNEY TEMPLE
CEO AT MONET MODELS / NSD PRIMERICA PARTNER

Q: You received the opportunity to compete on every level. What were your thoughts and feelings when you parted ways with life as an athlete?

A: "Athletics have always been a part of my life, so initially it was difficult to deal with. I played collegiately for Tulane University and Professionally for SSK in Feldkirk, Austria. Once I tore my ACL, I made the decision to end my career. Being a professional athlete was all I ever desired to become, but I am a God Fearing Woman and knew that I was talented in so many other areas. All I needed to do was redirect my focus. Fortunately, I was blessed to have found something that I enjoyed, almost as much, and that was modeling so I quickly redirected my focus toward pursuing a modeling career. Even though I was modeling, I was still close to someone who was playing professional sports and when I was upset about not playing, I felt like I was living vicariously through them."

Q: With time, you have become a very notable entrepreneur. What inspired you to keep dreaming in the midst of your transition?

A: "I knew that God had so much more than athletics in store for me, and that it was just the foundation I needed that would transition me into my real purpose; creating a business that can change the WORLD."

Q: What is your advice to young athletes who are afraid to dream after the disappointment of parting ways with sports?

A: "Realize that God is just getting started with you. Sports have prepared you for LIFE. You should use those tools you've learned from being an athlete; coach ability, mental toughness, teamwork, leadership, focus, hard work, and perseverance to become great at the new path God truly has planned for you. There is a beautiful world waiting for you to make your mark, all you have to do is have the same faith and confidence you had in your ability to play the sport you loved, and you can conquer greatness."

VANN MCCLOUD

ENGINEER

Q: Upon the disappointment of not advancing in your Pro Day tryouts, you returned to school to complete your education. How did you cope with transitioning from life as a student athlete to life as a traditional student?

A: "It was by no means an easy transition, the feeling of not having the same structure in life (being in the lime light) and daily schedule. Having more free time than I was accustomed too as a student-athlete, allowed more room for mistakes inside and outside of the classroom. I had to constantly remind myself that my task as an athlete was complete, and it was time to finish my duties as a student in life and in school."

Q: How did you utilize the cerebral skills that you obtained as an athlete to aid in your development as a young professional?

A: "Besides the technical knowledge I have learned through my degree, football shaped and molded me into the dependable, outgoing and dedicated teammate/co-worker I am today. The discipline I took from my athletic days has allowed me to understand what is to be expected of me as: a person, an employee, and a representative of my company. I have learned to take pride in my duties, as well as prepare myself for success, but never shy away from failure."

Q: What advice would you give young athletes who are in the process of evolving from their athletic career to a professional career?

A: "Remember that every situation in life is a business. If you don't put in work during practice, how can you expect playing time? Now that you are entering into a professional career, if you don't do what is expected of you as a professional, how can you expect to be paid or hired. Expect to receive, what you put in! For me, it has been a proven fact that the game is never won on game day; it's the preparation and practice leading up to the game that produces a win. So what you haven't made it as a big time athlete, life still goes on. Become a star in your own life. "STARS" are who they are because we as fans celebrate their actions and accomplishments. So do it for you and celebrate yourself into a star."

MARIO SPANN

RELATIONSHIP BANKER / YOUTH MINISTRY

Q: Upon completion of your undergraduate degree you were presented with several opportunities to pursue a career as a professional athlete, but you chose to take a different path. Why did your dreams change and when did you realize you were destined to do something other than sports?

A: "Growing up baseball was my passion and heart's desire.

93

For years I worked tirelessly to make my dream of becoming a professional athlete a reality but, the more I pursued it the further I felt away from God because baseball was my life. Everyone associated or defined me by the game and with that added pressure I began to lose myself. My relationship with the Lord is the most important thing in my life but the more I pursued baseball, the more I neglected that relationship and it began to show. I wasn't truly happy because I wasn't chasing after what God had for me; I was doing my own thing. My heart is in ministry and teaching others about Jesus. I pour my life out to others, so that they might know Jesus and it brings the greatest joy and excitement to my heart. No homerun, game winning hit or championship can even compare to that. It got to the point where I knew that to truly fulfill what God has for me, I had to stop playing baseball. There is no way I could effectively do what I'm doing for God now if I were still playing. Yes, I still would be saved and love the Lord, but my life would not have had as much meaning as it does now."

Q: Do you ever consider what might have happened if you had continued to pursue your child hood dream of becoming a professional athlete?

A: "Yes, at times I do think about what could have happened. But ultimately, I know that what I'm doing now is in the will of God for my life and I take comfort and peace in that. Baseball was and still is a passion that I have, I just don't play anymore."

Q: It seems that you kept an open mind and remained fearless to the unknown. What advice would you give to young athletes who might consider making similar decisions?

A: "We all have a desire within us to discover our purpose in life. I know that I want to fulfill everything God has for me and that caused me to evaluate who I was truly living for.

I'm not saying that you have to stop playing your sport to follow God, because that's not true. But search the one who created you to find exactly what is the purpose and reason that he designed you. That's the only way to find true happiness and fulfillment in life."

Epilogue

15 QUOTES TO REMEMBER

1. Talented athletes will work hard under supervised conditions, but great athletes will work hard when no one else is watching.

2. When you have learned to be a humble follower, it is then that you will become a strong leader.

3. Greatness is more than just a state of mind. It takes work to get there and it takes work to stay there.

4. When you give your best effort and it is not enough, determination will help you reload with the persistence that will allow you to endure.

5. Believing in yourself is the primary key to success.

6. Don't ever be afraid to step out on faith.

7. You are your biggest opponent. If you lose mentally, you will lose everything.

8. The challenges you encounter are only there to make you stronger.

9. The life you live can be defined by the type of risks you are willing to take.

10. Education is one of the most important tools that young athletes can obtain.

11. When you persevere through your hardships you will move to a higher level of achievement.

12. A young athlete who practices humility is one who has found a path to success.

13. Sometimes it takes a different kind of dream to make you smile.

14. God is writing our story and, to receive the full extent of His blessings, each chapter must come to an end.

15. As your pages turn in life, you have the God–given ability to turn with them.

Notes

Foreword by Tyrus Thomas

will. Dictionary.com. Dictionary.com Unabridged. Random House, Inc. http://dictionary.reference.com/browse/will (accessed: January 14, 2012).

Introduction

Nash, Jamia Simone. *Sometimes it takes a different kind of dream to make you smile.* "Raise It Up." August Rush: Motion Picture Soundtrack. CD. Sony BMG Music Entertainment, 2007. November 13, 2007.

Success is not measured by what you do compared to what others do; it is measured by what you do with the ability God gave you. "Zig Ziglar Quotes." Johnson, Keith. <u>The Confidence Makeover: The New and Easy Way to Quickly Change Your Life</u>. Shippensburg, PA: Destiny Image Publishers, Inc. 2006. 98.

Chapter 1: Youthful Thinking

Brown, Bruce. *The Odds On Becoming A Pro.*

Teaching Character through Sport: Developing a Positive Coaching Legacy. Monterey, CA: Coaches Choice 2003. Print.

CHAPTER 3: THE COACH

For what shall it profit a man, if he shall gain the whole world, and lose his own soul. The Bible: King James Version, Mark 8:36. *Editor's Name.* Red Letter Edition. *Nashville*: Thomas Nelson Inc., 2001.

Sometimes when you win, you really lose. White Men Can't Jump. Dir. Ron Shelton. Perf. Wesley Snipes, Woody Harrelson, and Rosie Perez. Twentieth Century Fox Film Corporation. March 27, 1992. Film

Your attitude, not your aptitude, will determine your altitude. Zig Ziglar. BrainyQuote.com, Xplore Inc, 2012. http://www.brainyquote.com/quotes/quotes/z/zigziglar381975.html, accessed January 14, 2012

CHAPTER 4: THE CHOSEN ONE

Faith is the substance of things hoped for, the evidence of things not seen. The Bible: King James Version, Hebrews 11:1. *Editor's Name.* Red-Letter Edition. *Nashville*: Thomas Nelson Inc., 2001.

As a mother, my job is to take care of the possible and trust God with the impossible. "Ruth Bell Graham Quotes." Canfield, Jack. Chicken Soup for the Mother's Soul: 101 Stories to Open the

<u>Spirits of Mothers</u>. Deerfield Beach, FL: Health Communications, Inc. 1997. 84.

Hard work beats talent when talent fails to work hard. "Taras Brown Quotes." Rios, Angel. "Kevin Durant: Hard Work Beats Talent When Talent Fails to Work Hard." MikesPickz.com. Web Solutions, Inc., 11 Feb. 2010. Web. 15 Jan. 2012 http://mikespickz. com/Sports/2010/02/kevin-durant-hard-work-beats-talent-when-talent-fails-to-work-hard-2/

Chapter 5: The Gambler

What great thing would you attempt if you knew you could not fail? Schuller, Robert H. "Robert H. Schuller Quotes." BrainyQuote.com. 2012 Xplore, Inc. 14 Jan. 2012 http://www.brainyquote.com/quotes/quotes/r/roberthsc107582.html

The Serenity Prayer

God grant me the serenity

to accept the things I cannot change;

courage to change the things I can;

and wisdom to know the difference.

~ Reinhold Niebuhr~

About the Author

TaRhonda White is a former two-sport student athlete who was born and raised in Baton Rouge, Louisiana. She earned a bachelor's degree from Southern University and A&M College in 2008, and is currently employed as a Nuclear Engineer. Additionally, she is the founder of Inspiring Dreams nonprofit organization and lives in Hampton Roads, Virginia.

For more information about TaRhonda or to schedule interviews, book signings and guest speaking appearances please visit:

www.tarhondawhite.com

Twitter Page:@TaRhondaWhite
Facebook Fan Page: Author TaRhonda White
Email: tarhonda@tarhondawhite.com